Perpetual Kindness

Creating a Global Movement Towards Love

I0139617

Perpetual Kindness

Creating a Global Movement Towards Love

Denise Walker

YouSpeakIt

PUBLISHING

*The Easy Way
to Get Your Book
Done Right*™

www.YouSpeakItPublishing.com

ISBN: 978-1-945446-29-0

This book is dedicated to my family: my mom, dad, three brothers, and seven nieces and nephews. Without them, I would not be the person I am today.

You are everything to me.

Acknowledgments

Thank you, Mom and Dad, Jean and Bill Walker, for being great parents and for teaching and modeling kindness throughout your lives. You mean more to me than I can ever express, and I can't thank you enough for your unconditional love and support.

Thank you also to my brothers, Todd, Curt, and Chad, and their wives—Kari, Kara and Pilar—who inspire me every day in their parenting of my nieces and nephews. Your work as parents keeps this kindness wave going. Thank you all for giving me comfort in knowing you are always there for me.

Thank you to all my friends who dreamed this dream before I did, believed in me, and continue to teach me that anything is possible, especially Darren Kaulius for lighting the fire under me to get started. Thank you to Jason Kurylo for always being there for me for the past twenty-five-plus years, and the many yet to come. Your friendship means the world to me.

And lastly, thank you to YouSpeakIt book creation and support teams. Without them, I would still be slogging away on my keyboard. Thank you for making this whole process easier than I could have ever imagined.

Contents

CHAPTER FOUR

CHAPTER FIVE

Introduction

Leave everyone you meet better than you found them.
~ Robin Sharma

Kindness: The quality of being friendly, generous, and considerate.

I wrote this book because a girl was bullied, and I didn't think it was okay. I didn't know this girl, but I couldn't believe that people's words and actions could lead to such drastic outcomes. It is unacceptable that atrocities continue to happen.

Our world requires us to band together in our common human experience to make a better place for us all. This world is not made up of you and me alone; it's made up of all people, interconnected and interdependent. And while this book is not about bullying and being bullied, if we are going to make it a better place, we need to acknowledge the role negative energy plays in taking away from kindness and happiness. We need to learn to recognize negativity in ourselves and others and change it where we can. We all need to do our part to create more kindness by being more kind to everyone *and* by being more kind to ourselves. We need this now more than ever.

It is my hope to create and inspire kindness that will eventually change our world. I think most people would agree that we could use more kindness, whatever that looks like to them. Kindness means something different to us all, so go out and do it, be it—because we can never have too much kindness.

I have worked in the medical community as a registered nurse for more than twenty years. I've seen firsthand how one kind word can change a life, just as an unkind word can. My life's work is to lead and inspire people to become reflexively kind, by creating more self-awareness of how one act of kindness really can have a profound impact on another individual and the world. I practice this in my daily life with my patients. I am also kind while speaking, to anyone who will listen to me. And while I am new at speaking publically on this topic, I am certainly not new at spreading kindness or acting with it.

It seems that kindness has become a forgotten form of public behavior that needs to be re-taught in order for it to again become a natural response; because we are actually born with a sense of kindness but the world we live in changes how we react to it.

We hear a lot about conditions that stem from a lack of kindness:

- Bullying and cyberbullying
- Anger
- Self-loathing
- Anxiety

By teaching and modeling kindness, we can significantly reduce these issues worldwide.

We can shift the focus instead toward kindness, acceptance and love

These qualities are what we need to send out to our world.

Perpetual kindness from one person to another can move other individuals to do the same, creating global movement. It is not enough to just *be* kind these days; we also need to *talk* about kindness, so that we can shift our awareness and make that change. We need to treat others with kindness so that they feel valued enough to pay that kindness forward.

Remember, often the people we find hardest to love are the ones who need love the most.

Being kind isn't hard, and it's often just little things that really make a difference in people's lives. You can have such a profound effect on somebody's life. We really need to take the time to be mindful of the things that we and other people say. The more kindness we put out, the more we will get back. The law of cause and effect states that what we put out is what we get back tenfold. This means that if you are angry, most likely your day will be filled with other angry people.

The beauty of that is that if we are going to put kindness out, we get ten times the kindness back. It would make for a nicer world. I urge you to keep that in mind as you go through your day. See what kind of a mood you are in, and what kind of mood the people around you display. See what and who you attract to yourself.

As you read this book, highlight sections if you want to, make a list of kindnesses you see throughout your day.

You will be amazed at how many there actually are and how many of them you can practice yourself:

- Make a list of kindnesses you see.
- Make a list of your own kindnesses.
- Photocopy the lists and hand them to everybody you know.
- Encourage others to do items on the list and add their own.
- Do something fun, and make kindness a game.

Being kind can and should be fun. It should be natural. I think all of us laugh and smile naturally, and being kind should be natural as well.

Being kind can be simple:

- Smile at somebody.
- Give somebody on the street corner a couple dollars.
- Say hello to someone you've never met before.
- Buy somebody a hot dog.
- Hold the door open for someone.
- Let someone in front of you in traffic.
- Compliment someone.

If I can leave you with one final message, it is: please, always choose kindness. We really have no idea the effect we have, and can have, on others just by being kind.

> *In a gentle way, you can shake the world.*
> ~ Mahatma Gandhi

Let this be our gentle way, and change the world together, one kind act at a time.

CHAPTER ONE

The Importance of Kindness (The Amanda Todd Story)

How wonderful it is that nobody need wait a single moment before starting to improve the world.
~ Anne Frank

My daughter and I were driving in Vancouver on a cold rainy night. We started to talk about how cold and miserable it was outside, and as we approached the corner of Georgia and Howe Street, my daughter noticed a man sitting in the pouring rain. She reminded me that we had a blanket folded up in the trunk of our car. It had belonged to my son when he was little and we now used it for outings at the park.

As we rounded the corner, my daughter said out loud exactly what I was thinking, "Mom, we should go give that blanket to the homeless man."

I thought about it and mentioned the blanket was sentimental and held memories for me of my son. We both decided that his memory would be honored by the blanket going to this man to him keep warm and dry.

We drove around the block. There were no spots to park the car, and it started to pour rain even harder. We ended up circling around three times. On the third attempt, we double-parked the car, putting our blinkers on. We quickly walked down the street toward the man on the corner. I bent down to give him the heavy quilt. He thanked us and we both caught a glimpse of his heart-felt smile as we walked away. When we walked back to our car, our arms around each other and the rain coming down hard on the umbrella, I teared up.

We realized the blanket wasn't a lot to give, but, to that one man on a cold winter's night, it meant a lot. A couple weeks later, I drove by that spot on the corner of Georgia and Howe Street and glimpsed the man sitting on the corner, bundled up in a blue patchwork quilt. I remembered how the act of kindness felt and how we were able to experience the act of giving.

~ r. g.

AMANDA'S STORY—MY CATALYST FOR SPEAKING ABOUT KINDNESS

I've been blessed my entire life. Let me just open with that. I've been fortunate to be born, grow up, and live in Vancouver, Canada. I have an amazing family. I went to private school, I now have a wonderful career, and I have travelled to many places in our amazing world. I have seen some beautiful and incredible things, and have the means to continue to see more.

In a conversation I had while writing this book, my friend reminded me that many of us are truly privileged, yet we don't realize it. *Privilege* does not necessarily mean that you are wealthy or middle-class. It simply means that you have rights, advantages, or immunities; having opportunities and resources available to you, which you may take for granted. A privilege can be where you were born and who you were born to, where you live, and access to necessities and everyday comforts such as clean water, food, shelter, and clothing. We have privileges in many ways that we don't even think about.

My blessings and my privilege include that I have had a standard set of parents, three brothers growing up, and a very idyllic life. I didn't go to high school. My mom was on the school board, and she didn't like the curriculum. She took my younger brother and me out of school when I was in grade seven. So, I never went to high school, and I never saw bullying. I got along with my brothers. We never fought or hit each other. I could not have comprehended or imagined that horrible stuff happens.

I am truly very blessed, and have led an easy life. So, when I see or hear things that are less than my ideal, I take note.

One of these things was a news story I saw a couple of years ago. It was a story about a fifteen-year-old girl, Amanda Todd, who posted a video on YouTube. The news story was about Amanda, her video, and the events that followed. After the news, I went to YouTube to check out her video, and I watched her tell her own story.

During the eight minutes of the video, we don't see Amanda's face. She has printed her story on pieces of paper, which she is holding up and flipping through one at a time. We learn that when she was in grade seven she would go on webcams with her friends, to meet and chat with new people. She was complimented on how beautiful, perfect, and stunning she was. One day a stranger asked her to "flash" her boobs. She did. My guess is that she was about twelve years old at that time.

There is no music (although it has since been added), and she takes her time flipping from one piece of paper to the next. For the next seven and a half minutes, we learn that one year later, she received a message on Facebook from the man who asked her to flash him. She does not know him. He tells her that she must "put on a show" for him or else he will send her picture to her friends and family. He knew where she lived and where she went to school.

Later that school year, at Christmas break, Amanda received a knock on the door at 4:00 a.m. It was the police, who informed her that her picture had been sent to everyone. For the next three years, she was bullied mentally, physically, and emotionally. She would go to school, and the kids would bully her. She would switch schools, and the same thing would happen again. She tried to commit suicide but survived, only to receive posts on her Facebook page saying, "I hope she's dead," "I hope she dies this time," "she should try a different kind of bleach," and, "I hope she sees this and kills herself." Finally, after three years, she had enough, and she posted her powerful video on YouTube. Shortly after posting that video, she did succeed in committing suicide.

For some reason, Amanda's story made a big impact on me. It really hit me. I hear about situations like hers all the time in the news; kids who are bullied as young as seven years old are taking *their* lives! I don't know if it was because Amanda lived locally, or because of her video, but I took her story to heart. It bothers me that things like that happen in our everyday world. It makes me wonder: *what is going on in our world?*

This book is not just in memory of Amanda and all the other people in our world who have been on the sad end of bullying, persecution, meanness, injustice, racism, anger, self-loathing, suicide, and any other atrocity, but to get people to be more mindful and to realize how simple it is to be kind, and to remind them that you really *can* change someone's life by being kind, just as you can by being unkind.

Moving Beyond My Bubble

Bullying happens. Not bullying alone, but people being unkind to others in general society. I have been fortunate enough not to experience a lot of that personally. When the reality of Amanda's story was placed in front of me on the news program, it opened my eyes to what is outside of my bubble.

When I move beyond my own safe home and family situation—my bubble, I see that life for other people can be unpleasant, unfair, and dangerous. One of the things that I remember journaling about after seeing Amanda's story is that I had such a feeling of heaviness. It breaks my heart to think that this is happening in our world on a daily basis. People can be so unkind, to the point that they cause others to take their own lives. That does not make sense to me, and it's not okay.

Amanda Inspired Me to Live My Purpose of Inspiring Others

Amanda's story was the catalyst for me to realize that *something needs to be done*. When I saw Amanda's story on the news, I could no longer pretend that bad things don't happen, and I had to *do something* about it. I don't know if it was because she was from the local community—I didn't know her. I couldn't pretend bullying wasn't there anymore.

My friend, Kimberly, once said to me, "Now that I know what I know, I could no longer pretend I don't know."

It's exactly like that for me now. I can no longer pretend that bullying, cyber bullying, gossiping, anger, unfairness, prejudice, racism, and more don't exist. I see and hear unkindness happening all the time, but for some reason, Amanda inspired me to speak up, made me realize that I can do something—I *have to do* something. I believe that those of us who have had a blessed and privileged life have a duty to lead others from this great position, to lead the world in whichever way we are called. We've been given that privilege for a reason, so let's use it. The more kindness we create and inspire, the bigger change we will create in our world.

PERSPECTIVE—IT'S EASY TO BE KIND

I think people believe it's hard to be kind and they can't trust kindness. But if we put into perspective how easy being kind is, and what a difference you can make for someone else, it will seem easier. My goal is to show people how easy it really can be and the difference you really can make in somebody's life just by being kind and doing one kind thing. We can't always know how our actions affect somebody.

Experiences of Kindness, Experiences of Love

Everybody has had an experience of kindness. But I don't believe that everybody has had an experience of love. Over the years, other people have challenged me on this. Some of those people have been abused, and they said they experienced love, but their definition of love was very different from mine. I maintain that even if you've been abused—mentally, physically, or emotionally—bullied, or assaulted throughout your life, when someone smiles at you, that is an experience of kindness.

I heard this great quote the other day, attributed to Lao Tzu:

> *Kindness in words creates confidence.*
> *Kindness in thinking creates profoundness.*
> *Kindness in giving creates love.*

The idea around this book, *Perpetual Kindness Toward Love, is exactly* that—the more kindness we have, creating these perpetual waves of kindness, the more it turns into love. My hope is that people will see that. No matter where you go or who you are, you have had some experience of kindness before. My goal is to help people create a wave of kindness and have that wave turn into love and have it be a nicer, kinder world with more love in it, so it is a better place to live in. Multiplied acts of kindness will eventually turn into love.

The Story of Mark and Bill

I tell the Amanda Todd story at speaking engagements. I initially take people through a closed-eye exercise like this one:

> *Envision that you are getting ready for a big event:*
>
> *You are wearing your best clothes. You've done your hair, or if you don't have hair, then you've shined up your head. You have sprayed on your favorite scent.*
>
> *As you are walking out the door, you catch a glimpse of yourself in the mirror and think:* I look fantastic!
>
> *You walk into the venue and see all the lights and the people. As you walk in, someone hands you a glass of champagne. Another person takes your coat. You walk farther in to check on the seating arrangements. You see that you are seated at the head table—not only that, but this event is held in your honor.*

From there, I ask you to open your eyes and listen to a story. I tell you about Amanda and her video.

Another story I include is one I read years ago by John W. Schlatter in *Chicken Soup for the Soul*. It is about a high school boy named Bill. It was a Friday afternoon, and Bill was carrying a load of books, along with the rest of his locker contents. He tripped over his feet, knocking all his belongings to the ground. Another student Mark saw what had happened, helped Bill pick up his belongings, and offered to carry some of them home for him. On the way, the boys talked, and eventually ended up at Bill's house. They shared a soda as they passed the afternoon watching TV and talking.

As their high school years went by, the two boys saw each other occasionally, and with three weeks left in their last year, Bill asked Mark if they might talk. Bill asked Mark if he remembered how they met years before, and told him that the day they met, Bill was going home to commit suicide—that after the short time and few laughs they shared, it was enough for Bill to realize that he would miss many more times like that, and thanked Mark for saving his life.

I use those two stories because it is really easy to see how you can change somebody's life with one kind word or act, just as you can with an unkind word or act. The stories show the impact you can have by doing something simple like picking up a book and giving it to somebody.

Driving and Waving

That last part about picking up a book and giving it to somebody is not a heroic act. Neither is holding the door open for the person who is right behind you, or letting that car go in front of you in traffic, or just smiling at someone because you don't know where that person is going or where that person is coming from.

Somebody recently sent me an email about a woman driving down the road with her boyfriend. The boyfriend would smile and wave at every person they saw.

After getting some strange looks and some waves back, the girlfriend asked her boyfriend, "Why are you doing this?"

He commented that he had recently read an article about a study on people who had tried but not succeeded in committing suicide. When they were asked what would have changed their mind on that day, many had said that if a stranger had just acknowledged them with a smile or a wave, they wouldn't have tried to end their lives.

So, he said, "I want to save a life today."

Now, I question whether smiling or waving at someone is enough to keep someone from committing suicide, but I like to think that maybe—just maybe—it gives someone hope for just a little while. These are very easy actions to take. It's not a massive feat to pick up a book or to smile at somebody or to give them a wave or to say hi. Kindness isn't hard.

At the end of my talk, I ask people to re-imagine the scene of the great gala event where they see all their friends and family and thousands of people they don't know:

Now I want you to go back to the image of that big gala event, the one with all your friends and family and thousands of people you don't even know, and I want you to look around the hall.

Now imagine that the gala is really just a gathering of all the people you have helped or made feel good by being kind to them. These people are all here because they felt your kindness.

All the people at your gala event represent ripples. I think of kindness as a wave. Every kindness that we do creates a ripple, and all those people represented your ripples from the kindnesses that you have done. Those ripples create a tidal wave that will eventually change our world.

TEACHING OUR KIDS KINDNESS WILL EVENTUALLY CHANGE OUR WORLD

I believe we are born with a sense of kindness, but the world we live in changes how we react to it. As we grow older, we get busier with life, and kindness gets lost. People don't think about it because they get caught up in their lives, but if we teach kids from the very beginning, model kindness for them, and actually talk about it, we help create the next generation of this kindness wave. Children are the ones who are going to carry that forward and pass it down to the generations after. We need to start encouraging kindness early because that will cause and support the shift.

Protecting Innate Kindness by Teaching and Modeling

I believe kindness is a forgotten form of public behavior that needs to be re-taught. The core sense of kindness we're born with is evidenced in the behavior I see in my nieces and nephews. I understand that my family is privileged, but I think all kids, regardless of their backgrounds, *want* to help, until they learn otherwise.

How many kids do you see picking flowers for Mommy, helping to sweep, or putting the dishes in the dishwasher?

This is our innate sense of kindness. Some might say that it is just the children mimicking their parents, but I think on a deeper level it is their sense of kindness.

My nieces are nine and seven. I asked them, "What does it mean to be kind?"

Without missing a beat, they said, "Helping somebody, maybe with their homework or something else. Sitting with them at recess if they have nobody to sit with."

They get it. Kids just get it. Children naturally want to help. We are all born with that innate sense of kindness and empathy. But as we get older, society taints us. We see and learn more about life, and our context changes.

In the media, for example, we see celebrities featured, often in unfavorable ways. Saying unkind things gets a big reaction, which translates into big ratings for radio, TV, and web presence. The more controversial and saucy the news, the more of an emotional charge, which means they get more viewers and listeners. Because it's so prevalent, we become desensitized to how unkind it is, and speaking disrespectfully about others becomes the norm.

One radio station I listen to has a bit called *Celebrity Sleaze*. They dish all the gossip on stars. Gossiping becomes the norm because we see and hear it happening all around us. Children are particularly susceptible to this. Look at teen magazines, which publish a lot of content that's hopeful and nice—fluffy stuff about lives of the stars and what they have done. Then, notice what appears in magazines for adults—a lot of garbage and gossip. Up to a certain age, we treat kids with kindness and focus on positivity. Then, BOOM—we treat them differently once they are older. I think of Miley Cyrus. As a child, she played the Disney character Hannah Montana, and everyone loved her. She is an adult now, older than twenty, and she gets picked on all the time. It's sad that this happens in our society every day, everywhere we look, yet we rarely give it any thought. It becomes the usual background noise throughout our day.

Our children are tuned into us adults and look toward us for clues of how to be. Every day we show them through our own actions what kind of behavior is expected and what is acceptable. We really need to support children so they don't change those genuinely kind thoughts as they grow older—so they know it's important to be kind, stay kind, and stand their ground. We need to teach them not to get caught up with the Hollywood gossip or whatever gossip is going around at that moment.

Children Are the Start of the Coming Shift in the World

Whitney Houston popularized the lyrics of Messer and Creed's, *"I believe that children are our future…"*

We are already born with a sense of kindness, so why not keep cultivating that?

Kindness has become a forgotten form of public behavior that needs to be re-taught. As a culture, we focus on difficulties, like bullying, cyber-bullying, anger, self-loathing, and anxiety, among others. The stem of all these conditions is rooted in a lack of kindness caused by thoughtlessness. We can encourage more self-awareness by teaching and modeling kindness. We can significantly reduce these issues worldwide.

You cannot do a kindness too soon, for you never know how soon it will be too late.
~ R. W. Emerson

My request is to send your ripples of kindness today, tomorrow, and every day. Talk to your children, family, friends, and strangers. Be a role model for them. It's those ripples that will eventually change our world.

CHAPTER TWO

Born With a
Sense of Kindness

*I've learned that people will forget what you said,
people will forget what you did, but people will never
forget how you made them feel.*
~ Maya Angelou

*I'm a southern girl, born and raised in Texas, now
living in Seattle (so I'm out of my comfort zone, to
say the least). I had a job that was downtown in the
middle of all the high-rise buildings and crowded,
bustling streets of Seattle. I was only about six months
into this new position and having a really hard time
connecting with the small team in my office. I'd been
trying to connect, but it just wasn't happening.*

*One day, the fire alarm in the tall building went off
and the whole building had to evacuate. Because of
the location of my desk, I didn't hear the alarm. After
some time, I did notice the silence but that wasn't*

new to me because my teammates often would all go to lunch together, leaving me alone. So, I sat there until the lights went out which finally clued me in to the fact that something wasn't right.

As I went in search of the others, I finally heard the fire alarms and knew I had to evacuate the building—down thirty-six floors. Walking alone down all those flights, the thought kept hitting me that I wasn't even memorable to my team. No one cared about me. No one noticed me. I had grabbed my bags and decided that I was going to catch the bus and go home. As I was waiting at the bus stop, a homeless man with dirty clothes, uncombed hair, and a beard came up to me. He offered me a beautiful daisy. I politely declined and explained that I didn't have any money with me to offer in exchange.

He said, "No charge. This one is on me. You look like you need this more than me."

In tears and with gratitude, I accepted his gift. I cried all the way home on the bus holding my beautiful flower in knowledge that I am cared for. That has been the greatest, most heartfelt act of kindness I've ever experienced.

~ Sara Lencho

KINDNESS IS INNATE

I've always believed that we are born with a sense of kindness, but the world we live in changes how we react to it. We have this sense until we are conditioned not to have it. I also believe that our practice of kindness comes from our sense of compassion, and that the two words are always linked together. Kindness is the end result of compassion.

Research Supports the Theory That Kindness Is Innate

In a study at the University of Wisconsin, psychologist Jack Nitschke showed what happens in the brain when we feel compassion. Parents had electrodes attached to monitor their brain waves as they were shown pictures of their children. When viewing a picture of their own child, the brain waves reacted, giving an indication of what it looks like when one is experiencing a feeling of compassion.

In one particular study, researchers added to the pictures of the subjects' children pictures of people who were in pain, obviously uncomfortable, or in some situation that didn't look very fun. Whether people viewed their own children, or strangers experiencing some form of trauma, researchers noticed the subjects' brain waves were the same. Everyone had the same sense of compassion. The science tells us that we are born with that sense of kindness and that it stays with us throughout our lives.

In my own research and observations, I have seen many people, children in particular, just wanting to help out and do things that are innately kind. I believe that people know deep down whether or not they are being kind, and it is my hope that people remember that we are born with this sense, and use it often. Some people call it intuition, or a gut feeling. We all possess the capacity to feel and thereby have the ability to know things without conscious reasoning. Our innate sense of kindness is run by our gut feeling, and we sometimes need a reminder to listen to it.

Personal Stories From My Nieces and Nephews

Children pay attention to everything we do from the moment they are born. I remember hearing somewhere that children learn more in the first five years of their lives than they do in the remaining lifetime. Regardless of whether this is true, there's no denying that the first five years of a child's life are fundamental. So, let's teach them right from the beginning.

We also have a lot to learn from the children around us. I am lucky enough to have seven nieces and nephews, and they are all amazing. From them I've learned many lessons about kindness.

One particular story I remember is about presence as a form of kindness. My three-year-old nephew and I were playing cards one morning. I had my cell phone with me, and it rang with a text message at about 8:00 a.m. I picked it up, read the message, typed a message back, and put the phone down. This took only about fifteen seconds.

My nephew—who, remember, was only three at the time—looked at me and said, "Auntie Neicy, aren't you forgetting to play with me?"

That story reminds me I need not to be busy and not be on the phone while I'm visiting with my nieces and nephews. Now, I never have my phone when I am with them. As I said before, kids just know. They still have that innate sense of whether someone is there for them, spending time with them, in the moment with them. Kids pay attention.

Sometimes we need a little help to edge past our own interests. One Halloween, I was with my three nieces as they went trick-or-treating. After they had finished making the rounds, the two older girls—ages eight and ten—wanted to share their candy with their friends. Their five-year-old sister wasn't very keen on sharing her candy with anybody, which is an understandable impulse for that age. I could see her watching her sisters closely. Because they were sharing, she pushed past her own desires and decided she wanted to share as well. Her sisters modeled kind behavior for her. She had no problem sharing her candy after that.

In a conversation with my nieces about kindness, I asked them whether they could be kind to somebody they didn't like.

They looked at me, nodded their heads, and said, "Of course you can, Auntie." For them, it was a no-brainer.

Kids want to do the right thing. They know what the right thing is for themselves, and they are so awesome and open that they just do it—they don't think about it. They don't think about what the world is telling them to do; they don't have all those influences and inputs that we do. They revert back to their sense of kindness.

Kindness—and Unkindness—Are Powerful

We all know what a gut feeling is. It's that feeling we can't push down, get rid of or ignore. Not unlike an alarm going off without warning, it tells us something is not right. It is a gut instinct that tells a mother that something is wrong with her child. Whether you are a mother or not, male or female, it is this, our internal radar, that connects us to one another and to the rest of the world.

As found in the study mentioned above, research done by neuroscientists shows that we all have a sense of kindness or compassion. Many people sense when they go against their nature; they feel uncomfortable. They feel it in their gut. We all have a gut reaction when we know we are doing something wrong.

When I was in grade four, there was a boy in my class I didn't like very much. I don't know why I didn't like him that much. He was the only adopted boy I knew, and that made him different. Back in those days, *different* meant *scary* to me, and I didn't know how to respond. I remember sitting with him on the tires after school one day. I knew my mom was coming to pick me up.

I remember thinking: *What is the meanest thing I could say to this boy?*

I thought it up, and then I said it.

To this day, when I think about that, it still bothers me. I was so cruel. Shortly after I said it, I ran away, and my mom came to pick me up. I got home and realized that I was so powerful with my words. I also realized that I could be really mean. I never wanted to be like that again. Perhaps that is why I am writing this book.

I knew that it was wrong. I remember how awful I felt afterward. Grade four was a long time ago, but I still feel bad about it. I knew I was being unkind, and it felt and still feels horrible. I reached out to this fellow on Facebook, and he hasn't accepted me as a friend. Maybe I'm still carrying that stuff around.

Did my comment deeply affect this boy?

I have no idea, but it's certainly affected me for all these years.

I knew at that moment that I was doing something wrong, and all these years later, I still know it was wrong. I knew when I was nine years old that it went against my gut, against my innate sense of kindness. I carry that with me to this day.

Think about something you've done that you know was unkind, for instance: have you ever wronged someone on purpose, said something unkind about someone or gossiped about them, lied, or were dishonest with someone?

If we are being honest with ourselves, I bet we could all think back to having done something like that.

How did you feel in that moment?

When you think back on it, do you get that gut feeling I'm talking about?

When we feel that, it bothers us. It's telling us we really need to listen, to get back to our sense of kindness.

Kindness is deceivingly powerful, yet we forget.

THE WORLD WE LIVE IN CHANGES HOW WE REACT TO KINDNESS

Every single action we take has consequences for other people and for ourselves, whether we are aware of those consequences or not. We see behaviors and situations, how people treat each other, and react to them. We create a judgment about them and react. Our reactions create results, but we are often not aware of the results that we get. I want to encourage people to be more aware of the things they are doing, how they are acting, and why. It all comes back to having a conscious awareness of the things that we do.

As an example, have you ever driven somewhere and once you've arrived, you have no idea how you got there? Do you have a regular morning routine that you don't have to think about? This is our *autopilot.* Do an experiment and ask your family or friends about some of your automatic behaviors. My guess is that you had no idea you did or do some of those things.

When we become aware of the things we are doing and not doing, that is when and where a change can begin to take place. Become more aware of the kindnesses you show and are shown, and it will show up more in your life. First consciously, and then, beautifully, unconsciously.

How Our Stories Become Our Beliefs and Truths

We tend to make judgments about each other and take action based on that judgment. It's easy to get stuck in the ego—we all do from time to time. Protecting the ego becomes our main concern and that decides for us whether we want to be kind or not. We're concerned about how it will look to help someone in need: will we look silly?

Eventually, the observations we make and the beliefs and attitudes we build become our truth, and our truth is closely tied into our ego. What we perceive as truth informs what we do next. How we treat somebody else is based on the story we've created in our head. How I feel about me determines how I feel about you. Yet, who am I to judge what my patient, client, co-worker, family member, or a stranger needs or deserves based on whatever story I made about them?

In some cases, we become jaded and worry that people are taking advantage of us. We don't want to look foolish and be taken advantage of. For me, I still sometimes struggle with the notion that I am being taken advantage of, and I become leery of what is being offered. I have learned that this is simply my ego getting in my own way of not wanting to look foolish. And what I know to be true for me is that I have missed a lot of opportunities because of this. The fear of being taken or looking foolish overrides my natural desire to help. That becomes a main focus rather than helping others. It's a shame that that is how we live and how our society is.

If we are more attuned to ourselves and our gut instincts, we can change this automatic feeling. People are only mean when they're scared. This means people get greedy and do things they normally wouldn't do, because they are scared of something. They end up bullying people in some way to either hide or suppress their fear. I attribute this to a *scarcity mentality*.

A scarcity mentality is simply the idea that if others have more than you, you do not have enough. It is the belief that resources—time, money, energy, jobs, houses, clothes, compliments, kindness—are scarce and that there's not really enough to go around. It is the idea that my human needs and desires will go on forever, but there isn't an infinite amount of resources to be spread around, and I'll miss out.

In my work at the hospital, I cover a lot of ground in a day. I'm often walking in the hallway. Whenever I meet a child, I offer them a sticker from the collection I carry with me. A few children refuse to accept a sticker. It appears to me that they are afraid to take one. I think these children are conditioned early to be wary of kindness, whether receiving or giving it. I find that to be a very sad situation, especially for a child to have learned this at such a young age.

You may also notice that this reluctance to accept kindness happens a lot, especially as we grow older. We become conditioned to reject kindness. We become part of a busy society and forget about our gut instincts, our primal impulse to be kind.

If I encounter someone being mean or unkind to me, my remedy is to be kind back to them. It throws them off. It's unfortunate that is how our society is, if we are kind to somebody, it might throw them off. People need to see that kindness so they may eventually become aware of their actions. Usually, people are being mean for a reason, and it's not me. It's because of their own issues, so I don't take it personally. They will realize or see how I am behaving, and eventually if they keep seeing kindness, they will get it. This is my hope, anyway.

Send some kindness back, and you will be that kindness that changes them.

OUR SENSE OF RIGHT AND WRONG THOUGHOUT OUR LIVES

I work with all types of populations in the medical community. I find it interesting that different age groups tend to relate to kindness differently.

I've noticed three groupings in my observations:

- **Children** are born with a sense of kindness, but they don't know it.

- **Adults** believe: *We need more kindness* but seem not to remember how to create more.

- **Seniors** revert to understanding we have a sense of kindness while actually knowing it.

A full circle is created.

Children

I recently saw a story on Facebook about a kindergarten teacher who brought her class two shiny, new apples. She got the children in a circle and told them, "These are two apples. This first apple, we are going to talk to this apple and tell it how much we love it. We'll say nice things like, 'how beautiful you are,' 'how shiny you are,' 'how pretty and red you are,' 'you're a perfect apple.' " The kids went around and each gave the apple a compliment.

She held up the second apple and told the children, "I want you to say something mean to this apple. Say, 'I don't like you,' or 'you're ugly,' or, 'you won't taste very good.' "

She went around the circle and got a response from each of the children, except for one. One little girl refused to be mean to the apple.

The children didn't know that the teacher had banged the second apple on the floor several times before bringing it in. It still looked beautiful on the outside, but she knew it was marred on the inside.

Now that they had said things to the apples, she cut them open. She cut the fresh apple open and showed them how pristine the inside was. Then she cut the damaged apple, and it was bruised—brown and mushy—on the inside. It was such an amazing visual comparison for the children to see: We may look the same on the outside, but on the inside, we could be carrying bruises. If you say mean things to somebody, even if they seem fine on the outside, they may be hurting inside.

I loved that story. It was so powerful for me. It was a profound lesson for these children to physically see that. And what about the little girl who didn't want to say anything mean? She knew it would cause harm. She couldn't bring herself to do something that may hurt someone or something else. As I've said before, children just know what's good.

Adults

When I tell people that I am writing this book or I am a speaker about the topic of kindness, they think it's great and say we need more. Everybody jumps on the bandwagon, which is fantastic. I love it.

I find it interesting that adults love the idea of focusing on kindness, but they don't think about it. The adults I've talked with know they need more, but sometimes, they forget that they, themselves, can model kindness and create more. It's my hope that people will understand that it's up to them to generate more kindness in the world. In fact, that's the only way to get more.

A beautiful thing is that there are more kindness organizations and events. World Kindness Day is on November 13, for example. These organizations get more adults and children involved. For the adults, organized events seem to be a good way to bring their awareness back to kindness. I can see a trend in teenagers starting that way as well.

We all have it in us to be positive role models for everyone we encounter.

Seniors

I love working with the old population. Twenty years working in medicine does that to you. Elders with cognitive issues are my favorites. For the ones who are confused with some form of dementia, I can't really say they are always kind because they are not. If they have fear, for instance, they can become self-protective or belligerent and be unkind. But for the most part, they still have a happy day.

Elders with age-related memory loss may have no recollection of who you are, as is the case with dementia, but they are still kind in the end. Seniors who are still lucid and fully cognizant look back over their lives and have amazing stories. They, like most of us, have been kind and unkind in their lives. They have been on the receiving end of both for various years. In the end, they understand they need to be more kind in order for our world not only to survive, but also for it to thrive.

I love the full circle. Kids are born with kindness, but they don't know it, and they cultivate it as they grow. As adults, we get forgetful about that. In the end, the elderly return to a state of understanding it. By then, a lot of people have families, and that becomes their focus. They are simply kind. They know that kindness is what runs the world.

Grandparents are the *everything* models for their grandkids. They do fun things with their grandchildren. My mom would bake and cook with her grandchildren, spending time and modeling that kindness without the kids being aware of it. The same is true for my dad, although he does not bake with them—he's very happy to eat all the cookies with them.

Adults need reminders to think about kindness, but once we get to the later stages of life, it becomes an automatic part of us once again. Grandparents are automatic role models without thinking about it. I just love how natural the cycle is.

We Learn to Forget

Sometimes we forget our innate kindness. We are born with that sense of kindness, and somewhere along the way, we get deconditioned, or forget to listen to our gut telling us whether we have done something wrong or what choice we should make. We need to be reminded that we do have a gut-level feeling of wanting to be kind. Some people call it *intuition.* We all possess the capacity to feel and thereby have the ability to know things without conscious reasoning. Our innate sense of kindness is run by our gut feeling. From time to time, we need more reminders. We need to listen to it more.

So, listen to it and be a positive role model for kindness wherever you go—whether it's the grocery store, school, work, or shopping—and notice the change in people around you. Become a conscious, positive influence on people because we all have it in us to do so. Become more aware of how you really can change someone's life just by being kind, and you will notice this difference. By being kind to others, you will create the change for other people to be aware of their kindnesses for other people. We don't want to wait until we are elderly or senior to become automatically kind. Start now. Start today. Start the ripples today and every day after that. Create those ripples that will eventually change our world.

CHAPTER THREE

Communication and Kindness

Today I bent the truth to be kind, and I have no regret,
for I am far surer of what is kind than I am of what is
true.

~ Robert Brault

The day is Tuesday, September 27, and I am now seventy-four! I go to knitting and Marilyn—who is sixty-six the same day—greets me, and we hug and wish one another happy birthday.

Brenda, our hostess, tells me that there is gluten-free cake for me, thoughtfully brought by Gigi, whom I also hug.

We happily knit together for the morning, and I leave to walk my dogs. Their exuberance and floppy-eared trotting beside or behind me always bring smiles to the faces of people approaching us. The dogs are my joy-makers, lifesavers, and my connection to the world.

I return home to do a few chores. Shortly after, Jo calls to sing Happy Birthday and ask how my day is going. This woman, who lives in Beaconsfield, Quebec, calls me regularly. She's a sixty-something-year-old woman who does landscape work with her daughter and is usually tired when she gets home. She's tired today, but takes the time to talk to me and check on how I'm doing. We remember our birthdays because they're exactly one month apart, hers being October 27. We talk until her son arrives home and she gets supper ready for them. She wishes me a wonderful dinner before hanging up.

It's about 4:30 by this time. Time is flying! I get the dogs' supper ready for them by 5:00 p.m. This is early, but I have plans to go to dinner at a favorite Greek restaurant. I've called and don't need a reservation. I ready myself and head out to the restaurant.

I enter the door and three staff (women) ask: "How are you doing?"

I answer: "I'm seventy-four today!" and ask for a window table.

My server is a sweet young woman. She takes my order. In the meantime, a male guitarist sets up and wanders up and down the restaurant aisles, playing soft, rhythmic tunes. What ambience! I've never heard music played at other times I've been at this restaurant, so this is special for me. Supper arrives. I finish what I can eat of my meal and ask for the remainder to be packed to go. I order an ekmek—a traditional Turkish bread pudding—and the server brings it with a candle flickering under the to go box. The fans above are blowing hard enough to make the flame almost go out and the box protects it enough to reach my table. I quickly blow it out with a birthday wish, and thank the waitress. The dessert is luscious.

A woman from three tables away approaches, asking: "I noticed the candle. Is it your birthday?"

I smile and say, "I'm seventy-four today!"

She says, "I'm seventy-five today!"

We exchange a few words, and she continues, "I notice that you are eating alone. That makes me feel sad."

"Don't be sad. I'm happy. I'm in my favorite restaurant, there's music playing, and the food's great!"

"What a great attitude! I'll leave you to your dessert. Happy birthday, again!"

"You, too. Happy birthday!"

I am blown away by this woman's positive attitude. She's with her son and daughter, forty-something people, who obviously enjoy the company of their mother. She's from Coquitlam, so she's come a bit farther than I for a meal at her favorite restaurant.

I finish my dessert, continue to listen to the guitarist, and wait for my bill. After waiting for a while, I ask my server, "Where's my bill?"

"Oh, you don't have to worry about it. It's taken care of."

"What do you mean, 'taken care of'?"

"Someone paid for your meal."

"Who?"

She pointed to the woman's table, "Her son and daughter took care of it."

Overwhelmed by their generosity to a stranger, I weep for a moment. The server notices and comes over to hug me. "These are tears of joy, Honey!"

She smiles, and I prepare to leave. On my way out, I stop at the birthday woman's table and ask the younger woman, "May I give you a hug? Thank you for such generosity!"

She accepts a hug, as does her brother, who had politely stood when I approached.

"We were glad to do it."

I thank the staff for such a nice evening, walk out of the restaurant, to where my car is six minutes past my metered time, and drive on home! While I would have like to have had my partner of nineteen years present and doting on me, that was not to be. I had a great time, because I chose to enjoy myself and witness the kindness of strangers.

~ Nettonya

SOCIAL MEDIA AND TECHNOLOGY MAKE IT HARDER TO COMMUNICATE

This morning I saw a graph of the frequency of the use of the word *kindness* since the year 1800. It spiked around 1830 and had declined steadily, dipping to an all-time low between 1980 and the year 2000. How interesting is that? Since 2000, it's been rising slightly.

Communication is the key to life, and if we don't have it, then we lose out on the experience of telling people how we feel and hearing how they feel. We are so caught up in our busy lives, and we are very busy texting or not talking to people face-to-face. That busy-ness leads us to become thoughtless in our everyday lives and actions. It's that thoughtlessness that is killing kindness. Kindness can disappear without those face-to-face everyday conversations and interactions.

Kids No Longer Communicate Face-To-Face

Technology is amazing. I happen to be technologically challenged, but I still think it's amazing. My five-year-old niece knows how to turn an iPad on while I don't. Technology has really helped us, there's no doubt about that—but at the same time, technology is changing so much of our world.

It takes people out of the game of life. Not that life is a game, but technology takes people out of living a shared experience. The generation growing up now has computers, internet, and social media. But one form of communication they don't get much practice with is communicating face-to-face. That is sad. I have heard of companies that offer communication courses for their new hirees because they don't know how to talk to people on the phone. It's crazy. We need to have more conversation and interaction time instead of spending so much time on social media.

When I go to a restaurant somewhere, and there are three people sitting at a table beside me talking on their phones instead of to each other, I think it's bizarre. It seems like most people don't interact in real time. That interaction is what we need in order to keep kindness going. Sure, you can be kind on social media, but it's not the same as having that physical, actual, heart-to-heart connection.

Texting Your Child's Wake-Up Call

I talked about kids earlier getting sucked into technology, but it doesn't only happen with kids. As adults, we buy into it as well. I text my fourteen-year-old nephew because it's easier to get in touch that way. I have friends who text their kids to get up in the morning, instead of walking upstairs and knocking on the door and having that face-to-face conversation. Now we don't have to do that.

When we adults use texting or other social media to replace conversation, we're teaching our kids to communicate like that as well. We're contributing to a new normal that includes texting rather than talking, even to people in the next room.

This needs to change so we can get back to actual physical conversations and being in the same physical location to talk with somebody instead talking over a device. It makes a big difference to see somebody and see how your words affect them. Maybe you can't know if you've hurt them because they interpret your text differently than you intended it. Maybe you've typed something in, tongue-in-cheek and laughing, but your friend has taken that comment seriously and it's hurting them. You wouldn't know because you can't see them. But if you are talking to somebody, you can see them react to what you say; you can respond in a conversation. Are they smiling at your comment, laughing with you? Or do they knit their brow or tilt their head in confusion?

As we spend time in society, we learn to ignore our innate sense of kindness. The new social norm becomes an *everyone-for-themself* mentality. We have become so busy in our lives that it is easy to be thoughtless in our actions, which internally causes us to forget about everyday kindness. You can see that happening anywhere that everybody is on their phones, not talking to one another.

The Ripple Effect of Being Kind

I have watched people talk about kindness for years, and what I understand from everybody is that the world really needs more kindness. For me, as I show people kindness throughout my day, I notice a shift in people. I notice that I really have a profound impact on people; I had never really thought about it before.

A colleague of mine had a bit of a potty mouth. With me being around, she stopped speaking that way. She noticed when I came in. I made it a point to say hi to her, and even if I was not in the same office as she was that day, I'd pop over and say hi. She'd seek me out as well, to say hi, and I noticed the impact that it has had on her.

Working in the medical field, I have been very humbled by seeing people at their most vulnerable and witnessing how they are affected by kindness. I have had patients come back to me and thank me for being kind to them and putting them at ease at a particularly scary point in their lives. It really has a profound effect on people when we are kind. And their kindness is returned through their compliment to me. Kindness really does come full circle. This stuff really works!

NEGATIVE NEWS AND REALITY TV

Much of the news is negative. Rarely do you hear the feel-good stories, the happy stories, the kind stories, the fun stories. It's mostly negative stuff: the wars, rapes, murders, kidnappings, elections.

For me, the messages are all fear-based:

- *Take this drug so you don't have a heart attack!*
- *Eat these foods so you don't gain weight!*

- *Buy this car to keep your family safe!*
- *Buy this health or airline insurance in case something happens!*

Fear is a huge motivator or driver for our society. The way the media portray fear as inevitable could keep people away from being kind to one another. They may worry that they look foolish or are being taken advantage of, as I said earlier. If we could live without fear—if we shunned this idea that we need to fear everything—huge companies would not have a stranglehold on us as a society, because we would not have a stranglehold on ourselves, preventing ourselves from doing the right thing.

We get used to living with fear because it's being marketed to us daily. Another way in which the media manipulates us away from our better natures is by marketing meanness. As an example, let's look at young singers and performers.

"Love Yourself"

There's a song Justin Bieber recorded that I think is really catchy. It's called "Love Yourself." I find myself singing it all the time. When I listened to it more closely, I discovered it's *not* a song about loving yourself in positive way, it's a scorned lover being sarcastic toward their ex. It's actually kind of mean.

This is not the only song that is catchy and popular but negative in its tone. I'm sure you can think of a few that have been popular. Sitcoms and movie plots can also be really negative. The effect of being exposed to negativity all the time is that we grow to accept it. We don't even bat an eye when we see cruelty on TV. It becomes the standard.

At school, there may be a kid who's being bullied and everyone knows it. We see it happen but hesitate to step in. We think: *I don't want to get in the way, or perhaps, this kind of thing happens all the time.* Maybe we see everyone else bully them as well, so we jump on the bandwagon instead of intervening.

In the media, we see bad things, and the energy around us becomes negative. Magazines use Photoshop to make stars appear with a certain body type, which then makes us feel like we need to look that way, too. If we don't, we think: *There must be something wrong with me.* We should learn to love ourselves.

Looking the Other Way

People are just so jaded these days; it is frustrating.

Why don't people help?

They think:

- *I don't want to get in the middle of things.*
- *I don't want to put myself out.*
- *I don't want to look stupid.*

A woman in New York City was being robbed, so this man went over to help her. He got stabbed in the process of saving her. She and the assailant both fled the scene. Meanwhile, the man who got stabbed fell to the sidewalk. A video camera recorded that he lay there for a period of *more than two hours*. People walked by and looked the other way, stepped over him, and did not offer any help. Nobody stopped to call 911. The man died.

It is so sad that our society is like that. We watch the news about the wars going on, injustice in the world, the deplorable conditions some people live in, refugees struggling to save their lives and families, movies, and so on. Nobody relates to them anymore because it is so prevalent. We become so desensitized that we don't think about these things anymore.

That is what needs to change. The more kindness we have, the more it will change. Perpetual kindness leads to love, changing the world.

Celebrity Bashing

There was a celebrity in the news recently who was the target of a home invasion. It was all over the news and, in fact, she got a lot of negative publicity about it. People judged her reaction as melodramatic and speculated about whether it really happened. Social media has made it so easy for people to be detached and anonymous, so they post things they would never say to anybody's face. If they had to say it directly to someone, they'd probably feel how mean it would be, or they'd worry about consequences. But in social media, and in today's society, it seems there are no consequences. So, this woman was bashed all over the media by naysayers.

On the other side of the camp, people were mad, wondering: *How could you say this stuff about her?*

She was scared for her life and didn't know if she would see her children again. I haven't seen her in the public eye recently. She was keeping a bit of a low profile. It's scary that social media has allowed things to get to this level.

Reality TV Isn't Real

I don't watch a whole lot of TV, and reality TV is my least favorite. It's not reality in any way, shape, or form. Things are so doctored on those shows to make them seem real, but I suspect what happens is that the producers often decide to pit people against one another to create the drama they feel will get better ratings. What comes across to the viewer is that we *hate* this person, or that person, which boosts the ratings, which earns more viewers and money, to make more seasons. We get caught up in the adrenaline hit in reaction to one person or another. This sells advertising, this increases profits, and it changes our society.

Then there are talk shows, like the *Jerry Springer Show,* that find people to come on and air their dirty laundry. People are selected specifically for that. It may get better ratings, but using a format like that also creates a lot of heartache and hurt.

These shows don't portray how life really works; it's not reality. But many viewers believe them. They think: *It's so real.* This belief continues to decrease our connection in the community and to one another. It helps us forget about what our everyday life is like. So, when we have a reaction to someone in our everyday life, we behave the same way we saw on TV, because that is the new normal.

Messages Come Through Whether We Know It or Not

We can hear and integrate messages without realizing it. Have you ever meditated with a guided audio? Some of them say things like, "I am great; I am loved." The idea is that while you're in a relaxed state, the messages will seep into your consciousness without you needing to do anything but relax.

Now consider what happens when you're relaxed, listening to music or watching a movie, or vegging in front of the TV when the news comes on. If you're listening to a kind of music that's angry, aggressive, or negative, those messages are going to seep into your consciousness. Say the news is on the radio in the background—some part of you hears those stories. We get input on a constant basis, coming in through our ears, our bodies, our eyes. It just becomes ingrained in us.

That is why we need to be, model, and create kindness so *kindness* can get ingrained in us. Not reality TV that runs on fear, not the big-money stories, not the big news. We need to stop buying into it. It needs to change. Maybe I live in a bubble thinking this way, but I want that bubble to expand.

WE CAN MOVE IN A BETTER DIRECTION

Kindness can create good ripples that we don't know about or see. The same is true of unkindness. I think most people can see how people who are cruel often create other people that are cruel—how the cycle of abuse is sometimes handed down from generation to generation in a family. If that first person could have been kind, the kindness would have rubbed off to the next generation, and so on. There are a lot of sad, hurt, angry, abused people. While kindness is a fluffy word, the effect it has is not. Because they have self-esteem issues, people are not kind. They use cruelty to help their self-esteem. Being unkind or cruel is the only way they know how to live, but the chain reaction can be broken by continuously being kind to that person, modeling it for them, and showing kindness to everyone.

What do I mean by breaking the chain reaction?

If one generation has no self-esteem, they are going to be cruel to the next generation and teach their kids to be cruel as well. The same is true of kindness. If you are kind, you are going to create a kinder generation, and that will continue.

You can break the chain of abuse. That is what I want to have happen.

We buy into the fear every day because we are surrounded by it in the news, magazines, books, and internet. Social media has made information very easily accessible, and the more we hear horrible stories of loss, violence, or meanness, the more we grow to expect it and accept it as normal. That is not good for our world, for our kids, for anybody. It needs to change.

How can we possibly make such a big change?

Let me share an example of a lifestyle change I recently made. I have been trying to get off sugar. I have been doing so well abstaining for the last six months, which is hard because sugar is in *everything!* I feel amazing having no sugar in my body, so when I had a couple of Tim Bits (yummy doughnut holes from a Tim Horton's shop), I woke up the next morning and felt like my body was poisoned. My body was not running how it should be, nor like it had been for the past few months. But prior to that, this feeling of unease, jitteriness, and being off kilter was the normal state in my body, and I didn't even know it. I used to not feel any difference in my body the next day after having sugar, but since I've been off it for so long, when I had some, I definitely felt it.

It seems a good analogy for when I am unaware of how things affect me: when I stop whatever that habit is, and then reintroduce it to my system, I definitely notice a difference, and it is the same with everything in life. Pulitzer Prize winning poet Mary Oliver's instructions for living life are, "Pay attention, be astonished, and tell about it." We must pay attention to the effects habits and choices have on us. That is the first step to create change—notice the difference; pay attention to how it feels. Because when we pay attention, we'll be astonished at the changes that happen, and the effect we really can and do have on others.

We need to get away from the media, TV, social media, news, and gossip outlets because they create a waterfall of bad effects. Those effects seep into our body. These messages come, and we have no filter for them. They are continuously poisoning our body because we keep getting exposed to them. We don't know how it feels not to have that anymore. That is the negative ripple effect.

This message needs to get out. It's not just about talking; we actually need to *do* something so the doing becomes the norm. Now that you've spent some time noticing what needs to change, and feeling what the change is like, it's time to act on it. There are many societies, people, and groups that focus on being more kind or more helpful. They help us put our ideas into action to create real change.

The Shift Back to Positive

A good step in creating change is to involve yourself with an organization that focuses on kindness: teaching, doing, and modeling it. One inspirational example is the Me to We

Foundation, founded by Craig and Mark Kielburger, two brothers in Ontario, Canada. When Craig was twelve years old, he was flipping through the newspaper, looking for the comics. He came across a story about a twelve-year-old boy from Africa who was involved in child labor. This boy from Africa was flown to the United States to receive an award. He spoke about child labor and its effects, was honored with the award, and then returned home. The news story Craig read reported that once back in his hometown, the boy was riding a bike with his cousin or brother, and he was murdered.

Craig read this and thought: *I am twelve, and he is twelve. But our worlds are a million miles apart.* He wanted to do something about it.

He went to his school and asked his class who would join him in doing something about this. Eleven other people raised their hands. They were eleven other boys who were all twelve years old. They created this group called "The Group of Twelve Twelve-Year-Old Boys." From that beginning group, the Me to We Foundation was born.

Their goal is to have the world change from a *me* mentality to a we mentality. This organization started as a few boys banding together to make a change in the world, and it has led to 2.3 million kids around the world becoming involved. WE Day is a celebration of all the work these kids have done. These kids want to be involved in their community and in a global project. WE Day is a big party to celebrate that. They get acknowledged for what they have done in the world and in their community.

You cannot buy a ticket to WE Day. You must earn it. Today there are fourteen WE Days around the world right now, in North America, Canada, and the UK.

One of the speakers at the most recent WE Day asked the audience, "What if the last thing you tweeted made it onto a billboard? What would it say? Do you want that out there, whatever you have just tweeted or sent a message about? What if it was the last thing you said?"

Think about that. Would you be proud of what you wrote? Good food for thought.

For those of us who use social media or are fortunate enough to have a blessed life, we have a responsibility to teach and model kindness.

A Kinder Reality TV

Not all reality TV is bad. In a show called *Undercover Boss*, a CEO, business owner, or high-position company executive goes into one of their stores undercover. They begin at an entry-level position to find out how the business runs, what can be improved, and, on a more personal level, who their employees are. With an altered appearance and a fictional story (to explain the cameras), they go to a different location every day, working in various areas and positions in the company.

At the end of the week, the boss returns to their real identity, and has a meeting with some of the employees they encountered during their experience. These employees are often given a gift of appreciation for their service, or perhaps they have gone through an exceptionally difficult time. The gift may be promotion in the company, training, material or financial rewards. It's such a feel-good show.

Another show is called *Secret Millionaire*. In each episode, the millionaire leaves their home and must live on a small budget (usually less than $150 per week), find their own accommodation for the week using this budget, and work and volunteer during their week away. They meet local people who are involved with community projects or something similar and help with these projects. On the final day, the millionaire reassumes their identity and surprises the people they've met with monetary gifts. It is usually thousands of dollars, and participants must donate a minimum of a hundred thousand dollars. What a great show, and a great example of kindness and how it has a ripple effect.

On one particular show I remember, the millionaire was based in a company in Seattle. The company used to have a big conference or gathering once a year, where he took his employees on a holiday. His secretary, his right-hand woman, had come to one of these conferences with her boyfriend. Somewhere along the trip, he had gotten a phone call saying there was screaming coming from her room. By the time somebody had arrived at her room, his secretary's boyfriend had killed her. He had no idea that she was in a domestically violent relationship. That really shook him, and spurred him on to realize he needed to do something about it. So, he applied for this show to help women who are in similar situations.

The producers of the show choose the city where the millionaire goes, and in this case, they sent the man to Las Vegas. He received one hundred dollars a week, all to cover rent, food, and any other expenses. He went to a café to get a drink. He noticed only women were working there.

As he spoke with them, one lady told him, "These are all women in a shelter, and they have been battered and abused. Our challenge is to help them get back into life."

He became heavily involved in helping the women's shelter, as well as with some other organizations he found while there. He now donates forty thousand dollars to their program.

These are the stories we need to see on TV. This is reality TV. Why can't we have this instead of the other stuff that pits people against each other? Fear, scarcity, and manipulation sell. Kindness needs to sell. How sad is that? We need to sell kindness.

My guess is that the people who are reading this book are already pretty kind. Remember, the people who have the greatest need for kindness are sometimes the hardest to be kind to. The people who are hardest to love are the ones who need love most. We get caught up in our own stories and forget this. Kindness is so empowering, and because of that, we need to extend it to people we judge as *less than* us, or as having a harder time than we do, or people who are addicted, or have other problems of some sort. We need to extend kindness, love, and compassion to people. Full stop.

You Can Disagree and Be Kind

Being kind doesn't mean we must agree with each other all the time. You may worry that you need to censure yourself in order not to offend someone who looks, speaks, behaves, or thinks differently than you. But the self-censure doesn't help—not others and not you. Keeping ideas bottled up doesn't lead to kindness. A greater kindness, both to the self and those we speak with, would be to express ideas that are true to the self while being respectful of differences.

True debate allows for a civilized exchange of ideas. But we rarely get to see examples of this. In the most recent U.S. presidential election, for example, candidates and their supporters resorted to bashing and insulting each other rather than listening to and responding to differences. Many political pundits behaved the same way, rather than engage in thoughtful conversation. The candidates are our leaders.

They set the example. If they are not rising to fulfill this responsibility, then it becomes all the more important for us to do so. We need to set the example of treating each other with respect and support others to do the same. If celebrities, politicians, and leaders would model kindness, then that will prevail. If they do not, it's up to us. As I've said before, I see this in my workplace: If people see you are kind to everyone, they will be kind as well.

If society sees you are kind to everyone, it will be kind as well. We really do have that ripple effect on people, even if we don't know it. Being kind to other people really empowers them to be kinder to others as well as empowering people to do greater things. When we are more confident, we go for bigger things. When we push ourselves further, we can further change the world with our ideas. You will never regret kindness.

CHAPTER FOUR

The Science of Kindness

Wise men don't judge: they seek to understand
~ Buddha

I was in a radio contest called "Survivor". We competed in rounds of tests or tasks, and the prize was a pair of tickets to see the band *NSync. Another woman was competing to win the tickets for her daughter, who wanted them so bad. *Her mom was working hard to win. I whispered to her daughter that if I won, I'd give them the tickets. The last task was to eat gummy worms in peanut butter. The mom was gagging because they were so hard to eat. I felt bad for her.*

I did end up winning and handed the tickets to the girl. It was hard for me to compete because I was recovering from an injury and I could not run for some of the challenges. I almost got voted off before the contest even started for this reason, but my good selling skills came into effect.

Later that day, after the contest was over, *NSync's manager made an announcement over the radio to offer me tickets and backstage passes to meet the band. He had heard about the kind gesture I had made for that little girl after going through the whole contest. I missed the announcement, because I had come into work late that day due to the contest and stayed late to make up for it; I didn't listen to the radio for the rest of the day. I heard about it on Breakfast Television the next morning.

I kept in touch with the family, and at the time I gave them the prize, they offered me the use of their cabin up in Whistler anytime I wanted. I never did take them up on it because I hadn't given the tickets in order to get something—the giving was the important thing. I saw how excited the girl was that her mom and I were the last two competitors. I also looked at how hard her mom busted her can to try to win it for her daughter. So, I felt more joy having the daughter go to the concert than if I had gone to it myself.

~ Celeste

WORDS SHAPE YOUR LIFE

Coming from a science background, I find it amazing the effect that we really have and we don't even know it. We are all molecular structures. Saying things—giving them voice—puts that energy into the universe and really has a profound effect. Therefore, we need to be conscious of the messages we are sending. In this chapter, I show you physical evidence of how the things we say really have an impact on the world. That is why we need to be speaking about kindness as well as practicing it.

I recently read an article about how words shape our life. It talks about two universal laws, the *law of attraction* and the *law of cause and effect*. The law of attraction is the belief that by focusing on positive or negative thoughts a person brings positive or negative experiences into their life. Or, to put it in another way, "Like attracts like."

Many years ago, quantum physics suggested that matter does not really exist. Everything is made up of energy that vibrates at a different frequency, and it is this frequency that forms all the creations we see. From this perspective, everything in life is an energy form rather than a collection of solid things. So, if we put out higher-frequency—more positive and optimistic—thoughts and feelings, we receive higher-frequency vibrations back. *And* if we stay aware of what we are putting out, we can control what we get back.

Universal Laws

There is a very popular book about this, called *The Secret* by Rhonda Byrne. In this book, the author claims that as you think and feel, you put out a frequency, and this frequency is sent into the universe. It attracts back to you events and circumstances on a corresponding frequency. As an example, if you think angry thoughts and feel angry throughout the day, you will attract events and circumstances that cause you to feel more anger. Alternatively, if you think and feel positively, you will attract positive events and circumstances. This suggest that such things as better health, wealth, and happiness can be attracted simply by changing your thoughts and feelings, which are automatically sent into the universe, and reflected back to you.

The universal law of cause and effect states that *nothing happens by chance.* Or, for every effect there is a definite cause, and likewise for every cause there is a definite effect. Simply put, you reap what you sow. Your life is shaped through specific effects caused by your thoughts, behaviors, and actions. If you are unhappy with the results, it is within your power to change the causes that created them.

What do I mean by this?

You can change your life simply by changing your thoughts, which may then lead to a change in your actions. And if you transform your thoughts, you can create a new destiny. Not just for yourself, but for those around you as well.

Such is the case of words; they too hold a vibration or energy, if you will. If you use kind and more loving words, they will transmit a higher vibration or energy into the universe, creating a higher vibration in general. You can use your words to uplift yourself, as many people do with personal affirmations. If you haven't seen the YouTube video with little Jessica doing her "daily affirmations" in front of a mirror, I suggest you check it out.[1] It is just priceless, and for me personally I can't help but smile, and think of all the things I am grateful for, just by hearing her.

Beware the Power of Negativity

Think of the last time you were with someone who complains all the time, or a *Negative Nelly,* as I call them.

How did it make you feel?

Did you feel uplifted?

My guess is no; and if you're anything like me, you're wondering how quickly you can remove yourself from the situation. That's what it's like being around negative energy. It's not only not fun, but it's also draining, especially if the person with negative energy is around you all the time. I've noticed if there is one complainer, there is probably another complaining with them as well.

---

1   youtu.be/qR3rK0kZFkg

It's almost as though they are in competition with each other:

"I had a terrible sleep last night. My arthritis kept me up all night!"

"Oh, at least you only have arthritis! I've had a migraine headache for the last week, *and* my arthritis medication is causing me insomnia on top of it!"

And on and on it goes. It's almost like a comedy act, if you can separate yourself from it.

Be careful with your words, and those you are around. They can and will rub off on you. I think the key thing is to be conscious of the words we are using. It is not just our conscious words that have an effect, but our unconscious words as well. In fact, I've read in several places that only 5 percent of our brains are conscious of the things we say and do. This means, that for the other 95 percent, we are living in an unconscious state; we do things automatically, without realizing it.

Remember the autopilot we discussed in Chapter Two? Think about how many times you've been driving in a car, arrived at your destination, and had no recollection of part of the trip. Or, how about the way you get dressed in the morning?

Many times we are on autopilot, and have no idea of the actual steps we've taken to get where we are. This is true in all areas of life.

You Build Your Beliefs Through Repeated Messages

The same article talks about the *illusory truth effect,* or just the *truth effect.* Wikipedia defines it as "the tendency to believe information to be correct after repeated exposure."[2] The repeated exposure can come from our thoughts, the news, radio, social media, and so on. The more we hear it, the truer it becomes in our mind.

How many times have you said to yourself something like: *It doesn't matter?*

That phrase definitely runs though my mind numerous times throughout the day. I might be going for an extra cookie, and tell myself one more won't matter, when in fact it does actually matter, to me—especially since I've had four already.

Or, how many times have you said things like, "I'm so stupid," or, "I hate my hair," or, "I'm an idiot!"?

Those words have a huge impact on your life, and once you continue to say them over and over, they are likely to become truth for you, and you start believing what you are telling yourself, even though it is not true.

The more you hear something, whether from yourself or others, the more likely you are to accept it as truth. This is the case with all the kids who are bullied. They start believing what others are saying, even though what they are hearing is

---

2   en.wikipedia.org/wiki/Illusory_truth_effect

not the truth. These words bring negative energy into your vibrational field and affect you on a physical and emotional level, and can and do have detrimental effects.

The more often you are exposed to something—a word, phrase, or behavior—the more your brain looks for evidence to make it true. Our brains do this by searching for patterns and consistency to make sense out of everything around us. This becomes a problem because a weak message, shown only a couple of times, will become more valid in our brains than a strong message, shown only once. It is this repetition that has the power to change our minds. And if we are constantly sending messages of fear, bullying, and unkindness into the world, it's no wonder that this is what prevails.

But here are some simple steps you can take to change all this, using the power of positive energy for good:

- Send thoughts of gratitude silently to yourself and aloud to others.

- Stop making negative comments to yourself and to or about others.

- Commit simple acts of kindness.

- Surround yourself with positive people.

Rhonda Byrne wrote another book, called *The Magic*. It is essentially a workbook that takes you through twenty-eight days of conscious gratitude. It prompts you to focus on something different to be grateful for and an exercise for each day. It is a very powerful book because it teaches you to be conscious of how gratitude changes your world. *The Magic* can be summed up in that one word: gratitude. Imagine the change we can achieve when we become conscious of all the positive words we use.

How can we not create a tidal wave of kindness by changing our thoughts and words, which will eventually change our actions?

CONNECTED BY WATER

There is a lot of water around us. As a human, depending on whether you are an infant or a full-grown person, your body is made up of about 50 to 78 percent water. That is a lot of water. The earth's surface is 71 percent water, and the air around us, according to scientists, is between 3 and 4 percent water. That also depends on where you are measuring the air percentage because you could be in a desert where it is 0 to 1 percent, or a rainforest or jungle where it could be up to 90 percent. There is a lot of water around us, whether it is in our bodies, the air, or the land.

According to a Japanese doctor named Dr. Masaru Emoto, we have a significant effect on the water around us. Water is the most prevalent thing around us in our world. Water is everywhere.

In the 1990s, Dr. Emoto performed a series of experiments on the physical effects of different stimuli on water, which was then frozen. The resulting crystals were photographed in their frozen state. He documented these crystals and the differences in their structure, which appeared to change whether they were labeled with words, prayed over, placed in the presence of music, or set in a specific environment.

To study the effects of words and ideas, he took two jars of regular tap water, and on each jar he wrote a word. I don't know what his initial words were when he started, but he usually used opposing words. He wrote the word *love* on one jar. On the other jar, he wrote the word *hate*. He put those jars in the freezer. He had photographers take pictures of the resulting ice crystals. He repeated the experiment with a number of different words. Some of the other words and phrases he used were *You make me sick and I'll kill you, Thank you, Adolph Hitler, and Mother Teresa,* things like that. He compared ice crystals from before and after the water had been prayed or meditated over.

The photographs showed astounding differences between the crystals. You can find them online on YouTube. A lot of people have done their own experiments to see if they get similar results. You can try experiments, too. Another way of testing the impact of sending your intent to a substance without the need of special photography or a microscope is to put equal amounts of leftover cooked rice into identical jars. Label one with a positive message and the other with a negative message. Each day for a month, take a few moments and feel your written message and direct that message toward the rice in that jar. Compare the two jars as the month goes by.

Results of Ice Crystal Experiments

Dr. Emoto's results were quite amazing, actually. In the love/ hate experiment, when he photographed the *love* crystals, they were beautifully shaped and formed crystals. The *hate* ice crystals were very deformed and misshapen. It warranted him to do other experiments, things like *You make me sick* and *Thank you.* The *You make me sick* crystals were disorderly, and the *Thank you* crystals were symmetrical, patterned crystals. The *Hitler* crystals were, again, totally deformed and misshapen, as opposed to the *Mother Teresa* crystals, which were beautifully shaped. Dr. Emoto's whole hypothesis was that the energy we are putting out has an effect. If we are putting out negative energy, we have a negative effect on the water that is around us. Just as when we put positive energy out, it has a positive impact.

When Dr. Emoto was conducting his experiments, people questioned him. They commented that the images could have resulted from the bias of photographers, but Dr. Emoto had written things in a language the photographers didn't understand. For example, he wrote Thank you and You fool in German, and the photographers didn't understand what they were reading. They could still see that the You fool crystals were misshapen and deformed, and the Thank you crystals were beautifully shaped. It was really amazing.

EVIDENCE THAT KINDNESS MAKES A DIFFERENCE

Why should we pay attention to ice crystal experiments?

I spoke about the ripple effect of kindness early on. We really have no idea how much effect we have on things because we can't often directly see it. Obviously we don't see molecules floating through the air, but the energy that we do put out is the energy that is perceived and the energy that changes the world. If we put out more kindness and we talk about kindness more than bullying, violence, racism, or whatever other bad stuff is happening in the world, kindness will prevail; the same way we talk about those other things so much, those things end up being what prevails. From Dr. Emoto's studies, it is very clear to see that when we put good energy out and raise our own vibration, it has a profound effect on the molecules around us.

We are putting our energy into the water, whether the water is in our bodies, the air, or the environment around us. We have the ability to shift that energy from negative to positive. I was thinking about it earlier as I was driving into work today. If you are around people who have been bullied, abused, or have negativity around them, you have no choice but to take that energy in because the percentage of water in your body is so high. It's really easy to see how people can get into that negative mood or have that negative energy around and carry it with them. Through the experiments of Dr. Emoto, we can see proof that we, as beings made mostly of water, take that energy on, and it has a profound effect on us.

If you are always barraged by messages like *You're bad, You're not good enough, You're ugly, You're stupid,* and so on, eventually it gets into your own molecules, your system. That becomes what you think. Don't believe everything you think. When you hear this negativity all the time—not just personal negativity, but negativity coming through the media as well—it has a massive effect on you. It has an effect on all of us.

That is the energy shift that I believe we are capable of changing in the world right now. It's negativity and fear, and we need to change it.

The Results That the Energy Shift Will Create

If you put out better energy, you are going to contribute to the creations of a more positive, kinder world. That is my hope, you could say, but it is already scientifically proven. This is scientific energy. We can hold it, we can feel it, and it does make a difference. When you put energy behind your words, it creates more positive energy. Likewise, when you support your actions with your speech, you generate more positive energy.

I want you to imagine now what happens when you are not the only person focused on kindness, but one of a sea of people focused on kindness. I am reminded of events that were tragic, yet afforded people the choice of how they would cope and help each other. I think of the tsunami in Thailand a few years ago and the hurricanes that have happened throughout the States, and the way in which these disasters have brought people together. It's bringing people together that creates that energy shift.

If I were to make a guess, even after 9/11, I would say after those events, as tragic as they all were, people felt good about banding together and helping others. I just saw a documentary about the 9/11 rescue, narrated by Tom Hanks, available on YouTube.[3] It talks about how about five hundred thousand people were evacuated from Manhattan in eight hours, and compares that to the 339,000 evacuated from Dunkirk over the course of nine days during WWII.

Some of the people interviewed afterward were the boat captains who came back continuously for people. They said things like, "I really made a difference. I just wanted to help."

After these *bad* events, people band together, and it creates a shift of people pulling together to help each other. People feel so good afterwards. If we could do this every day, not just when bad things happen, that would be enough to shake the world, to change it.

---

3   youtube.com/watch?v=MDOrzF7B2Kg

I think that it's all good and well to talk about things. Even for me, I get tired of listening to the fluff. *That's so nice. Oh sure, change the world, blah, blah, blah.* But this is actual science. This is science-based. It's not just fluff or woo-woo. It's physical evidence. As I said, you can see it, you can hear it, you can taste it. There's physical evidence that we really can change the world. It's important because the world needs to change. We can see this evidence, and we can see the difference that we make if we just look for it.

The Science Behind Kindness

Orly Wahba is the founder of the nonprofit organization Life Vest Inside (lifevestinside.com). Their mission is to empower and unite the world with kindness. Orly, a former middle school teacher, is the founder and speaks around the country about the Magic of Kindness, which is also the topic of her TED talk. Life Vest has put up an amazing video on YouTube called *The Science of Kindness.*[4]

In this video, they explain that, like prescription antidepressants, kindness stimulates *serotonin*. Serotonin is a hormone that helps relax you, heals your body, and makes you happy. When I act kindly toward you, it increases the serotonin in my body, and for you, as the receiver of that kindness, the serotonin is also increased in your body. What is really cool is that the people around us that have witnessed

_____
4   youtu.be/FA1qgXovaxU

the kindness also have their serotonin levels increased. That means that in the aftermath of a traumatic event, such as the natural disasters I talked about earlier, when people are helping each other, serotonin increases, and people are in a better mood afterward. They are kinder, friendlier, and more helpful, because of that higher serotonin.

This video also relates how kindness spreads to three degrees of separation. If I am kind to you, I have just affected three other people, and so on, and so on. That is a big effect that we have on somebody.

Imagine how many people are affected after a big event— how many people came together for the tsunami?

Endorphins are released when we are kind. Endorphins are naturally occurring chemicals produced in our bodies, and they act like natural painkillers. In the video, they talk about how endorphins are three times more potent than morphine. In my work as a nurse, I've seen a lot of people take morphine, whether it's by that name or a different prescription painkiller. Our natural endorphins are even stronger than those pharmaceuticals.

Kindness also creates a hormone called *oxytocin*, which is a hormone that gets rid of the stress in your body.

It's a scientific fact that being kind is better for your body and better for the world. I like facts, and I like science. I like seeing evidence. There is a lot of evidence as to how being kind has an impact on the world around us.

How the Energy Shift Will Change the World

In science, you can dispute facts, and you can come up with your own experiments and theories. In the end, I don't think anybody would say that being kind is going to have an adverse effect on anyone or anything around them. It will change things for the better: better energy, a better outlook, and a better output. People will become closer and strengthen the bonds with others.

I live in Vancouver, and there are a lot of people on the corner asking for money. There is this one guy named TJ. My guess is that he is in his fifties. He is about six feet tall, has a toothless grin and had throat cancer. He sometimes has his cat, Freddy, with him, and sometimes not. TJ stands on the same corner every day. I talk to him and give him gift cards or money. I stop to talk to him when the light is red or just wave as I am driving by, yelling out the window, "Hey TJ," it brings a smile to his face. It's hard not to smile when someone acknowledges you. I think a smile is a very good clue of somebody's happiness. The more we make people smile, the more positive energy that there is in the world. And if nothing else, it's a good place to start.

It's that positive energy that will change the world en masse. Those are huge events that I talked about earlier—the tsunami, 9/11, hurricanes Katrina and Sandy—they had a significant impact on the lives of people in the areas where they happened.

The fact that people come together and help create a change to help fix a problem creates a huge impact on the world. I'd like to see that as a lasting impact, so people are happier longer on a more continual basis. I know it sounds like I'm looking through rose-colored glasses, but I think we can do that if we are more conscious of the things that we are saying and doing.

When we are very busy talking about racism, bullying and violence, that is the energy we are putting out. Remember the water molecules, and how they changed depending on the words that they were labeled with? That is why it is so important to be talking about kindness so we can have kindness prevail.

CHAPTER FIVE

The Business of Kindness

Tenderness and kindness are not signs of weakness and despair, but manifestations of strength and resolution.
~Kahlil Gibran

After carpooling to a kayak race, I mentioned to my boss that my old car needed new tires and brakes, but that would cost more than the resale value of the vehicle. He asked, "What size tires?"

"14 inch," I said.

"I have some under my back stairs you can have." he said. "My son put brand-new tires on his car, but then moved out and bought a truck. He donated the car to charity years ago, but took the new tires off. It looks like they are the right width too."

He explained that brake shops require clients to replace the calipers to guarantee their work, and replacing or turning the rotors as well. He could replace the pads and shoes for his mechanic's discounted parts price, plus whatever I could pay for labor.

I had done some brake repairs on a previous car and realized that my skills are not great in that area. To make it a win-win deal, I paid the higher labor cost from the range he quoted. Now my ride is safe again, and that is due to the kindness of my boss.

~ Tom

SELF-CARE IS KEY IN LIFE AND BUSINESS

When you have a good sense of self-awareness and self-care practices, it is easier for you to bring kindness to other people, whether it's in the everyday world or in your work. For instance, if you spend a lot of time at work, make it a kinder place, you can have a better, healthier work atmosphere and look forward to going to work instead of dreading it. You'll find the kindness affects those around you: employees, colleagues, and clients. I think most people would rather have a kinder atmosphere around them.

However, kindness has to start with the self.

The Research

Through my research over this time, I've found a great flow chart that illustrates the way to happiness. It's by Carol Preibis, and it stresses the importance of being mindful of yourself.

Being mindful of yourself leads to three avenues, which ultimately all lead to happiness:

- Compassion for the self
- Compassion for others
- Appreciation

Compassion for the self leads to care for the self, like having a regular routine, having a meditation practice, talking to somebody, going to the gym, or going for a walk. In a way, it is showing love for yourself, the way you might love and care for a child.

Another path to happiness is by having compassion for others. Everybody has gone through traumatic experiences, and you might not know what they have gone through. But you can still feel empathy for them and concerned for their welfare. Having compassion for others leads to a sense of *altruism*, or acting unselfishly for the benefit of others. Having a sense of altruism leads to a state of happiness.

The third route to happiness mapped by Priebis is *appreciation*. When you cultivate gratitude or appreciation, you are putting that energy into the universe. What you put out is what you get back. Having more appreciation or gratitude keeps us mindful of how blessed we really are for what we have, whether it's a family, a job, a relationship, food, shelter, clothing. Being appreciative brings you to this state of happiness.

When you are in a better state of mind or a better place, it is much easier for you to be kind to those around you or in your workplace, which is where many people spend a lot of time. So, it's important to have that state of happiness and give out that kindness at work.

Working With Like-Minded People Creates a Better Atmosphere With Ease

When I bring my good energy to work, I notice there is a shift around me that happens. Thing are lighter when I get there. I feel like a rock star when I go to work because people are genuinely excited to see me. I love that. I get fed by that at work, and I am able to turn that around toward my patients and give them a big reception to make them feel special and at ease during their visit. That's the energy I send out, so it comes back to me tenfold. Like attracts like.

> *If you want happiness for an hour—take a nap. If you want happiness for a day—go fishing. If you want happiness for a month—get married. If you want happiness for a year—inherit a fortune. If you want happiness for a lifetime—help others.*
>
> ~ Chinese Proverb

If I am putting out good vibes, people are going to feed off me, and in turn, I am going to feed off them. When I encounter people at work who are cranky that day, or maybe they have gone through something that I don't know about, I know if I go in with a happy heart and I am joyful, it really changes the atmosphere.

I challenge you to be mindful of what you are putting out because you do get it back. Even if you are at a coffee shop or grocery store, be mindful of the energy you put out. If you have good self-care and self-compassion practices, it makes it easier to go out into the world in a happy or kind frame of mind. Practice that kindness and create the atmosphere you want at work and wherever you go.

THE MAGIC EFFECT OF BEING KIND TO YOUR EMPLOYEES

If you want a business that is profitable and successful with happy employees, being kind to your employees is key. There are so many benefits to being kind at work. The magic is in the results that kindness creates.

The Law of Attraction for Finding and Retaining Employees

If you are looking for kind-hearted, happy, healthy employees, it's really important for you to be those things yourself. I know there are a lot of studies and thoughts that if you are a nice boss, your employees are going to walk all over you, and you won't be as effective, and you won't be as accomplished.

But in fact, if you are a hard-assed leader, you might inspire a lot of resentment. I see it in my work and elsewhere, when I talk to friends about their jobs. If you put up a hard front, people don't feel comfortable coming to you. In the end, it takes a big toll on people when their experience of work is that their boss is a bully or is not caring.

From personal experience and my research, I've found that people are much more productive employees when they are excited to go to work and feel like managers and supervisors are supportive and approachable. Their professionalism, employee satisfaction, work performance, and creativity increases. Sick time decreases. They make better decisions and have better relationships.

How is your work experience affected by your higher-ups or boss?

Might it change if you felt the boss was kinder or more supportive?

I've noticed when I work with people who I feel are supportive, collaborative, and would bend over backward to help me, I am much more likely to be the same toward them. It's much easier to do work in an environment in which you feel appreciated and encouraged.

Better Relationships

Now imagine that you are the employer or manager, with a team of people working for you.

Are you sending positive or negative energy into the workplace?

What difference does it make?

People are in a better mental, physical, and spiritual state if they are in a state of happiness or have more kindness around them. They will go the distance for you because they see you are willing to compromise and work with others. You have created a positive atmosphere. They'll take fewer sick days, which means the company won't have to pay for sick leave and overtime to replace those people. Your workers will be in a better mindset when they go to work, with increased happiness, increased health, lower blood pressure, and lower cortisol levels. Burnout will be less of an issue. When workers feel good about their jobs, typically they have more energy. Maybe they are sleeping better because they are not as stressed thinking about work. These are all benefits of being kind.

When you create this kind of environment, you magically attract the type of people you want to work with or have work for you in your company or your business. You engage your employees more, and they want to do more for you. When employees feel appreciated and valued, they give more. I believe this is the way to run a business. If you want to have a successful business, if you want to make a profit and have successful projects going out, then being kind to your employees is the way to go.

Kindness Ripples Beyond the Employees

The kinder you are to your employees, the harder and better they will work. It carries over to your relationships with customers, clients, or patients, as well. When you treat your employees kindly, they, in turn, will be kinder to your clients, and your clients will be more loyal. They will want to stay with you as their lawyer, banker, or production company. Not only that, but if your clients, customers, or patients have favorable interactions with your business and are happy with the services or products you provide, they will be more likely to tell their friends about the great deal or the wonderful service they got.

THE BOTTOM LINE OF BUSINESS

Money seems to be the bottom line for a lot of companies in the world. So, let's consider the financial benefits of kindness in your workplace. As we've already established, happy employees stay in a position. If you retain your employees, you don't have to keep retraining numerous employees coming in. Kindness will increase your profits and decrease your operating costs because you don't have to retrain new hires; your employees will want to be there. You can divert that money into marketing or back to your clients, saving you and them money. Kindness is a win-win all around.

I was reading an article in *Forbes* that discussed a study conducted by the Jackson Organization about the top voted One Hundred Best Companies to Work For. The study said, that according to Dr. Noelle Nelson, author of *Make More Money by Making Your Employees Happy,* through employer kindness, companies' stocks rose 14 percent over a period of six years, as compared with 6 percent in the companies lower than the top one hundred.5 I found that interesting. These are definite, hard numbers that show how being kind to your employees does benefit your company and your atmosphere. It really creates magic.

I wouldn't say I am more attuned than the next person, but I am very grounded. I do know I love to be surrounded by magic. Kindness is magic to me. It works magic everywhere I go around the world.

When we become mindful of our thoughts and of the thoughts of other people around us, whether it is our family or our barista or our coworkers or our boss or our clients, when we become mindful, amazing things happen. We become more in tune with what is happening around us. We become more in tune to some of the experiences that those other people around us have gone through that we would not have given a second thought to before.

It's Okay to Care

Whether it's in life or in business, it's okay to care. It's absolutely okay to care. People are not going to think you are a softie because you care about them. People are going to look at you as a more approachable person, human being,

---

5   Cooper, Steve. "Make More Money by Making Your Employees Happy" Forbes.com (July 30, 2012).

boss, mother, or father. By caring, you are opening yourself up more for people to come to you and they feel comfortable doing that. In doing so, whether you are an employer or employee, whether you are running the employees or working for your customers or clients, the more open you are, the more kind you are, the more people you will draw toward you. It's a win-win.

I was reading a story about the CEO of a company. Apparently this company has a policy that when one of their employees has something happen to them, whether it's a loss or an illness or something else, the CEO actually gets the message and sends a personal message to that employee. The story I was reading was about this woman who had developed a brain tumor. Within fifteen minutes of receiving this news, the CEO sent a message to this employee asking how they can help. Even talking about that right now, I am choked up.

How amazing is that? Who doesn't want a boss like that?

You could be a boss like that.

Conclusion

Wherever there is a human being, there is an opportunity for a kindness.
~ Lucius Annaeus Seneca

I no longer run a business, but after interacting with people for forty-some-odd years, and meeting and seeing all types of people at their most vulnerable every day in my twenty-year nursing career, I know that people recognize and appreciate kindness. They feel safe with kindness. They want kindness. I have yet to meet one person in this world who does not like or want someone to be kind to them.

Perhaps you know someone like that?

If you do, be kind to them anyway, because you will never regret being kind.

Kindness can be done anytime, anywhere, and it can be done so easily. Kindness starts at home. Home might be in our actual home, but most of the time, it is in our heart.

We must be kind to ourselves before we can be kind to others. If you cannot be kind to yourself, it is much harder to be kind to others and accept kindness from others. Remember, the people who are hardest to love are the ones who need it the most.

The way to create a tidal wave of kindness throughout the world is by committing multiple acts of kindness, each day, with each person we encounter. All these small actions build together and create a huge ripple to counteract the political turmoil and wars. Start getting people involved in your communities. Get a group together. Give homeless people coats for the cold winters. There are so many things you can do out in your community getting people involved, and people are so excited. A lot of people are already starting the process of getting more people on board with kindness.

I am competitive. I like to keep track of things. If you do, too, you can make it into a game with your friends. See who can do the most acts of kindness in a day. This is also a great way to bond with your family. If you have kids, make it a family game—get them talking about the kind acts they did that day. Make a graph everyone can see and track how many kindness acts they did in the day, week, or month. Make it fun.

I started the book with the Amanda Todd story to illustrate how easy it is to change somebody's life with one kind word or act, just as you can with an unkind word or act.

I often wonder: What if somebody had just said something kind to Amanda right before she decided to end her life. Would that have made a difference, changed things, or prolonged her life?

I don't know, but I like to think it would have made a difference. It makes me happier to think that way; if I'm happier, I'll go about my day happier, be happier and kinder to those around me, and I'll have started those ripples of kindness across the world.

There is a sign at work that says:

It's not big to make people feel small.

People who bully others were most likely bullied too. People who are violent are often the victims of violence themselves. That is what they grew up with, and what they learned from the adults around them. That is what they know. The way to break the cycle of abuse is to be kinder. Remember: the people who are hardest to love need it the most. If we can just be kinder to everybody around us, the after-effects can be amazing.

One of the ladies at work said, "I was driving the other day, and this guy totally cut me off. I was ready to give him the finger, and I honked the horn at him. As he drove by, I realized it was one of my coworkers. Now, we just laugh about it."

I said to her, "What if you had known it was him before he cut you off? Would you have let him in?"

She said, "Yeah, totally."

Why don't we live our whole days like that, thinking everybody is somebody that we know, or maybe care about?

How much of a difference would just that one shift in our thinking, create in our day and our energy?

If we become more conscious and put more good thoughts, actions, vibrations, and words into the world, things will change naturally. Our mindset is everything. We get stuck and caught up in the negativity because there is so much of it around us, but that's simple to change. Don't let thoughtlessness kill kindness because you are so busy that you just go about your day, stuck in your own world. We need not to revert back to our regular thoughts, programming, upbringing, and context of life.

Sometimes there are lessons and good outcomes when bad things happen—the kind of learning that might not occur from what you'd consider to be good. Some might even say that struggle and challenge need to happen in order for us to grow. My hope is that we don't have to wait for something bad to happen for us to band together and make the world a better place. We need to help each other. We are all in this together. We are all in the same boat, in the same world. There is only one world, and billions of us.

Why not do our best to put good energy, vibes, words, and actions out there?

Throw those kindness molecules out there, and let them penetrate each other and permeate and wash over us. Together, we can change the world. It can be one person at a time, but we definitely make a difference.

You cannot do a kindness too soon, for you never know how soon it will be too late.
~ R. W. Emerson

Never let it be too late.

Next Steps

Go to perpetualkindness.com, where you will find blogs, stories of kindness, kindness quotes, and more.

About the Author

Denise Walker resides in Vancouver, Canada, where the weather is mostly cooperative with her love for cycling. She has volunteered for a number of organizations over the years, including Rotary International, Canuck Place Children's Hospice, and the BCFF Burn Camp. This is her first book.